Friends In Deed

OTHER BOOKS IN THE *LIFE'S GOLDEN RULES SERIES*

BOTTOM LINES - *The Golden Rules for Executive Success*
IT TAKES TWO - *The Golden Rules for Marital Bliss*
GROWING THEM UP - *The Golden Rules for Being a Great Parent*
PERSONAL FINANCES -
    The Golden Rules for Making The Most of Your Money
SINGLE PARENTING - *The Golden Rules for Raising Children Alone*
FRIENDS IN DEED - *The Golden Rules for Lasting Friendships*
SPECTACULAR SUNSETS -
    The Golden Rules for Making the Most of Your Golden Years
HERE I STAND - *The Golden Rules for Surviving a Breakup*

L I F E ' S G O L D E N R U L E S ™

Friends in Deed

The Golden Rules for Lasting Friendships

GENERAL PUBLISHING GROUP
Los Angeles

Copyright © 1994 by General Publishing Group, Inc.
All rights reserved under International and Pan-American Copyright Conventions. This book, or
any parts thereof, may not be reproduced in any fashion whatsoever without the prior written
permission of the Publisher.

The Life's Golden Rules™ series is published by General Publishing Group, Inc., 3100 Airport
Avenue, Santa Monica, CA 90405, 310-915-9000.

Library of Congress Catalog Number 94-078945
ISBN 1-881649-14-8

10 9 8 7 6 5 4 3 2 1

Colby Allerton, Editor
Cover Design by Nadeen Torio

PRINTED IN THE USA

Friends In Deed

1 ⋆ Friends are a gift to ourselves.

2 ★ Enjoy the simple things together.

3 ★ Jealousy is not a friendly trait.

4 ★ Cheer on your friends' accomplishments.

5 ★ Forgive.

6 ★ Laugh together.

7 ★ Lend a helping hand.

8 ★ The best way to have a friend is to be one.

9 ★ Never measure how much you give or get.

10 ★ Offer to baby-sit.

11 ★ Learn to listen.

12 ★ Each day we all face similar difficulties
with hearts that need friendship.

13 ★ Friends are there for the good times
and the bad.

14 ★ Keep your friends' secrets.

15 ★ Be friendly to yourself, then you can be friendly to others.

16 ★ Whenever confronted with the opportunity, be generous with heart-felt praise and encouragement.

17 ★ Why is it sometimes difficult to utter kind words to those we love the most? Say them, say them, say them.

18 ★ "I can live for two months on one good compliment."

—Mark Twain

19 ★ Friendship is acknowledging that we are separate people, and celebrating it, while striving to close the distance.

20 ★ There is mystery to friendship—and after exploration you may find yourself.

21 ★ Friendship is not just words, it is deeds.

22 ★ Friends know when to let you be alone.

23 ★ Friends "expect" nothing but friendship.

24 ★ Be willing to try new adventures together.

25 ★ Share your dreams and confide your wishes.

26 ★ Friendship makes defenses unnecessary.

27 ★ Friends know well each other's strengths
and weaknesses.

28 ★ Friendships find distance and time no real obstacles.

29 ★ Separation and even death must be accepted to feel the full richness of a friendship.

30 ★ Friends aren't always together.

31 ★ Friends don't always feel deeply about things.

32 ★ Friends do let you down.

33 ★ But that doesn't mean they love you any less.

34 ★ The main work of friendship consists of homely tasks—such as bracing each other up to face the unfairness of existence and getting through the tough times.

35 ★ "Give what you have. To some it may be better than you dare to think."

—Henry Wadsworth Longfellow

36 ★ You do not have to be a special person to be a good friend.

37 ★ Realize that you, and all others, are unique and lovable.

38 ★ Anyone can be a one-in-a-million friend!

39 ★ The best of friendships exist between people with flaws and shortcomings.

40 ★ Narcissism has no place in a true friendship.

41 ★ The best friendships do not require that anyone keep the upper hand.

42 ★ Real friends don't have to do much—there should be a simple, quiet joy in just being together.

43 ★ "That best portion of a
good man's life—his little,
nameless, unremembered,
acts of kindness and love."

—William Wordsworth

44 ★ True friendship is not a one-way street.
   If it is, it won't be one for long.

45 ★ Friendship, like marriage, may not be
   exciting unless you make it exciting.

46 ★ Do unto others as you would have
them do unto you.

47 ★ Dare to talk about your affection.

48 ★ "If you wish to be loved, love."

—Seneca

49 ★ Friendship is a privilege.

50 ★ It takes a deliberate effort to nurture an authentic interest in others.

51 ★ Start believing in people.

52 ★ Give compliments freely.

53 ★ Tell your friend, "You're beautiful."
A good friend will know you mean it.

54 ★ Work at being a helpful, considerate person.

55 ★ Be a friendly ear.

56 ★ "Give every man thine ear,
but few thy voice."

—Shakespeare

57 ★ Just be there to care, whether you know
what to do and say or not.

58 ★ Be supportive.

59 ★ Be able to withstand a good friend's
    occasional bouts of instability or
    irrationality.

60 ★ Real friends will help you through the
    rough times.

61 ★ Albert Schweitzer said, "We are all so much together, but we are all dying of loneliness." Reverse this feeling by reaching out to others.

62 ★ Always treat others as equals.

63 ★ Never label anyone—you may have just
missed an opportunity for a great
friendship.

64 ★ Laugh as easily as possible—it's much more difficult to keep muscles tense than to relax them.

65 ★ The happiest people do not have to push and shove.

66 ★ Look out for number one, but realize
how valuable it is, and how good it can
feel, to be willing at times to be number
two for a friend.

67 ★ Being a better friend helps make a
   better planet.

68 ★ Just thinking about friendship can improve it.

69 ★ People have a longing for relationships and
a desire for freedom: The best friendships
have room for both.

70 ★ Accept changes in each other's lives.

71 ★ In friendship, there is a large margin for error and a great need for patience.

72 ★ Friends are not just people with whom we share activities. They are people who, quite literally, let each other be.

73 ★ Friends don't take advantage of each other.

74 ★ Friends don't ask for too much.

75 ★ Friends find a way to thank you and
return the favor.

76 ★ Friends give each other enough time and privacy to continue their own special relationship.

77 ★ Friends accept each other as they are.

78 ★ Express your feelings clearly and honestly.

79 ★ Be willing to make compromises.

80 ★ Friends aren't afraid to ask for favors, but they don't impose too often.

81 ★ Never ask a friend to do anything you wouldn't be willing to do yourself.

82 ★ Feed your friends' pets when they are away.

83 ★ Help when your friend is being abused. Offer resources.

84 ★ Volunteer to drive.

85 ★ Be patient.

86 ★ Thank-you notes are a touching sign of true appreciation.

87 ★ Take pictures.

88 ★ A friend won't talk badly about you to others.

89 ★ Choosing friends for what they can do for you usually leads to disappointment.

90 ★ It's better to have one true friend than many acquaintances.

91 ★ Know the difference between friends and acquaintances, and work on both.

92 ★ "A friend to all is a friend
to none."

—Aristotle

93 ★ Listen carefully and try—especially when it is difficult—to understand.

94 ★ Accept and empathize if you can't understand. Maybe later you will.

95 ★ A good friendship is like a scratch for every itch.

96 ★ Friendship is the "inexpressible comfort of feeling safe with a person."

—George Eliot

97 ★ Make new friends, but keep the old. One is silver and the other gold.

98 ★ There is nothing as special as an old friend.

99 ★ Friends can last a lifetime if you work at it.

100 ★ A friend doesn't have to say what a friend she is.

101 ★ Include your friends in your plans and in your victories.

102 ★ Hop on a bike and take off on an adventure together.

103 ★ Never forget a birthday.

104 ★ Bring chicken soup when they're sick.

105 ★ Be on time, but be understanding when they aren't.

106 ★ Call if you're going to be late.

107 ★ Respect your friends' privacy.

108 ★ Respect your differences.

109 ★ Take an exercise class together if that
        makes the difference in going or not going.

110 ★ Offer to shoulder some of their
        responsibilities when they're sick.

111 ★ Small things aren't worth arguing over.

112 ★ Share your beauty tips.

113 ★ Don't have unreal expectations—friends can't solve your problems.

114 ★ Good friends don't give each other guilt for not calling.

115 ★ Friends are like rubber bands: They can bend without breaking and always snap back to their original shape.

116 ★ Good friends shouldn't make unrealistic
demands on each other.

117 ★ Don't overburden your friendship with too
many problems.

118 ★ To see a perfect friendship in action,
watch the Mertzes and the Ricardos on
I Love Lucy.

119 ★ Friends emphasize each other's good
qualities, not their flaws.

120 ★ A friend's honor is worth defending.

121 ★ A good friend will find the time.

122 ★ But respect their need for their own time.

123 ★ Friends are not threatened when you change or go in a different direction.

124 ★ A friend will tell you if you're on the wrong path.

125 ★ Do not expect your friends to do anything you wouldn't expect of yourself.

126 ★ Friends do not deceive us.

127 ★ If you lie to a friend, you lie to yourself.

128 ★ Don't choose a friend for what he has, but rather for what he is.

129 ★ All friendships change, to some degree, after sex.

130 ★ Friends can stay friends after sex, but beforehand accept the risk that accompanies it.

131 ★ "Friendship always benefits; love sometimes injures." —Seneca

132 ★ Play fair.

133 ★ Never steal a friend's lover.

134 ★ Fix your friend up on a date. But only with
someone you respect.

135 ★ Introduce your friends to each other.

136 ★ We do not possess our friends.

137 ★ Diversity makes friendships interesting.

138 ★ All friends help us remember where
we came from.

139 ★ Go the extra mile.

140 ★ It takes work to be a friend.

141 ★ "A real friend is one who walks in when
the rest of the world walks out."

—Walter Winchell

142 ★ Friends at the office can make some bad jobs better.

143 ★ Work friendships can be deep and satisfying.

144 ★ Work friendships may be fleeting.

145 ★ Don't let competition jeopardize friendship at the office—be teammates.

146 ★ Have a pen pal.

147 ★ Pets make great friends.

148 ★ Children make great friends. They teach us how to play.

149 ★ "A friend is someone who likes you."
　　　　　　　　　　—Charlie Brown, *Peanuts*

150 ★ "There can be no friendship where there is no freedom. Friendship loves freedom and will not be forced up in straight and narrow enclosures."

—William Penn

151 ★ Encourage positive change.

152 ★ Respect each other's choices.

153 ★ Avoid comparisons.

154 ★ With a good friend, few words are
necessary to say what you mean.

155 ★ Never give up the comfort of an old friend
just for the excitement of a new one.

156 ★ "Be slow in choosing a friend,
slower in changing."

—Benjamin Franklin

157 ★ "Keep well thy tongue and keep thy friends."

—Geoffrey Chaucer

158 ★ A friend doesn't speak for or about you.

159 ★ Tell your friend's secrets and you'll lose a friend.

160 ★ Never discount someone's feelings.

161 ★ Always weigh the consequences of your behavior towards your friends.

162 ★ Avoid the temptation to take advantage of a friend's good nature or generosity.

163 ★ When friends borrow money from each other it should be treated as a business transaction.

164 ★ Give it a lot of thought before you go into business with a friend.

165 ★ "When a friend deals with a
friend, let the bargain be clear
and well penn'd. That way
they may continue friends to
the end."

—Benjamin Franklin

166 ★ Friends should sometimes indulge each other's neuroses.

167 ★ Find the ways to provide the best support during a tragedy.

168 ★ Be the first to offer blood if your friend goes in the hospital.

169 ★ Encourage your friend to see a doctor if you think it's necessary.

170 ★ But avoid the Devil's advocate syndrome—even with good intentions, you may become a terrible nag.

171 ★ Don't give guilt.

172 ★ Love and support your friends.

173 ★ A good friend says what must be said and knows what not to say.

174 ★ "We discovered a terrific four-letter word for psychotherapy: talk."

—Penni and Richard Crenna

175 ★ Most people have at times felt inadequate
as a friend.

176 ★ Nobody's perfect, but simply the initiative
to improve makes one a better friend.

177 ★ Go to the movies and share your popcorn.

178 ★ Invite a friend along for the holidays.

179 ★ Shop together so you know each other's likes and dislikes.

180 ★ When you notice something positive, let them know.

181 ★ Never hesitate to tell someone how much you value their friendship.

182 ★ Actions speak louder than words (but it's still nice to hear them).

183 ★ Have respect for each other's opinion.

184 ★ Be sensitive to your friend's feelings.

185 ★ Be willing to be vulnerable.

186 ★ "Never close your lips to those to whom you have opened your heart."

—Charles Dickens

187 ★ In friendship, hearts relate to each other.

188 ★ A good way to deepen a friendship is to eat meals together.

189 ★ Exchange meaningful books.

190 ★ Have long talks.

191 ★ Friendships get closer in direct proportion to the amount of self-disclosure we volunteer. Open up to grow and feel connected.

192 ★ Friends can break our hearts better than anyone else.

193 ★ If you betray a friend, you betray yourself.

194 ★ Friendship—both great and small—offers durable strength in an increasingly fast-paced and deceptive society.

195 ★ Know when a friend is being two-faced to you and immediately call him on it. Life is too short and friendship too valuable to allow the undermining of a manipulator.

196 ★ "A man must eat a peck of salt
with his friend before he
knows him."

—Cervantes

197 ★ During a fight, talk about your feelings, not the other's faults.

198 ★ Aim for ventilation, not conquest.

199 ★ You can love and be angry at the same time.

200 ★ Apologize when you're wrong.

201 ★ Don't let hurt or resentment fester and
boil over. Talk about it.

202 ★ The restoration of a friendship will never
happen automatically—both parties
must choose to work it out.

203 ★ True friends deserve a second chance.

204 ★ "And if a friend does evil to you, say to him, 'I forgive you for what you did to me, but how can I forgive you for what you did to yourself?'"

—Friedrich Wilhelm Nietzsche

205 ★ When a friend weathers a particularly rough time of yours with no gain of his own, recognize that you've found and can cherish an irreplaceable true friend.

206 ★ "In prosperity our friends know us; in adversity we know our friends."
—John Churton Collins

207 ★ "If I had to choose between betraying my country and betraying my friends, I hope I should have the guts to betray my country."

—E.M. Forster

208 ★ Allow yourself the luxury of hugging or
      touching a friend—everyone should be
      able to enjoy a warm embrace.

209 ★ If you buy friends with gifts,
      it's like stealing.

210 ★ "The only gift is a portion of
thyself."

—Ralph Waldo Emerson

211 ★ Give of yourself every day, not just when there's a crisis.

212 ★ It is harder to be a friend than an enemy.

213 ★ Every person has something interesting about them if you're willing to look.

214 ★ The possibilities for personal joy and
fulfillment are endless when you take the
initiative and decide to be a friend.

215 ★ No one has to be alone.

216 ★ The ability to make friends takes a willingness to appreciate what is good in another person.

217 ★ New friendships and old friendships begin again all the time.

218 ★ Friends come in all sizes, colors and religions. Be careful not to hastily rule anyone out.

219 ★ Smile—you just might make a new friend.

220 ★ Don't let a failed friendship make you gun-shy about forming new ones. No one should be afraid to love.

221 ★ Look for friends with common interests.

222 ★ Always look for new and interesting
friends in new and interesting places.

223 ★ A hello to a stranger can start
a friendship.

224 ★ "You can make more friends in two
months by becoming interested in other
people than you can in two years by trying
to get other people interested in you."

—Dale Carnegie

225 ★ Friends are made, not born.

226 ★ Look for the things you like about a
     person—not what you don't like.

227 ★ Take up a hobby with a friend.

228 ★ "All men have their frailties;
and whoever looks for a friend
without imperfections will
never find what he seeks."

—Cyrus

229 ★ Establish a goal of making new friends wherever you go.

230 ★ Call a friend today.

231 ★ Express interest in the things that interest them.

232 ★ Give your time.

233 ★ Be compassionate.

234 ★ Friends inspire one another.

235 ★ Be a friend to yourself.

236 ★ Respect each other's differences.

237 ★ Be only as critical as you would want
others to be of you.

238 ★ Look for ten good qualities in each friend.

239 ★ Allow your friends to be themselves.

240 ★ Defend your friends, don't condemn them.

241 ★ Loyalty is essential.

242 ★ Avoid making promises you can't keep.

243 ★ Don't break the ones you do make.

244 ★ Friends should feel they can be honest
without recrimination.

245 ★ "Friendship without self-interest is one of the rare and beautiful things in life."

—James Francis Byrnes

246 ★ Choose your friends wisely.

247 ★ Hugs sometimes work when words
fall short.

248 ★ Learn to put yourself in a friend's place.

249 ★ If you are a happy person, you make a
happy friend.

250 ★ Learn to be flexible.

251 ★ Friends don't compete.

252 ★ Envy is an evil trait.

253 ★ "Friendship consists of forgetting what
one gives and remembering what one
receives."   —Alexandre Dumas

254 ★ To be a friend is easy when someone's down, a key is to soar along when a friend is flying high.

255 ★ Enjoy your friend's success.

256 ★ Avoid trying to pull others down.

Friends In Deed

257 ★ Everyone—especially our friends—
should be allowed to flourish

258 ★ Let your friend's success inspire you.

259 ★ Know that friendship relies on much more
than accomplishment.

260 ★ Don't meddle in your friend's business.

261 ★ Gossip only hurts your friendship.

262 ★ Friends are not afraid to admit their faults.

263 ★ Friends share their shopping secrets.

264 ★ Friends really don't care what you look like without your makeup.

265 ★ Friends look after one another.

266 ★ Good friends can be depended on—always.

267 ★ Give a friend a ride home.

268 ★ Treat him to lunch for no reason.

269 ★ Be a friend to those less fortunate.

270 ★ Be a phone friend to someone who is ill.

271 ★ Your faith is your friend.

272 ★ Charitable acts are friendly acts.

273 ★ Do nice deeds. Don't just talk about them.

274 ★ "We secure our friends by not accepting favors, but by doing them."

—Thucydides

275 ★ Go out of your way for a friend.

276 ★ Let little annoyances go by.

277 ★ Be tolerant.

278 ★ Be polite.

279 ★ Think before you act.

280 ★ A sharp tongue does not make for a smooth friendship.

281 ★ Talking badly about your friend's family can be a dangerous sport.

282 ★ All actions have consequences.

283 ★ Avoid the mistake of taking out your
frustrations out on your friends.

284 ★ An occasional note or letter is most
appreciated.

285 ★ If a friend needs a lengthy explanation,
supply one.

286 ★ A good sense of humor will come
in handy.

287 ★ Try to soothe an aching heart.

288 ★ Everyone has misunderstandings.

289 ★ Follow a friend's good example.

290 ★ "The best way to cheer
yourself up is to try and cheer
somebody else up."

—Mark Twain

291 ★ Friends encourage each other to try new activities.

292 ★ A good friend won't tell you you're too old for anything.

293 ★ Friends care about how we really feel.

294 ★ Friends don't abuse each other.

295 ★ A friend is not afraid to say when they've been hurt.

296 ★ Cheer for your friend to win.

297 ★ Good friends don't forget to say "thank you."

298 ★ True friendship comes when you respect the other person's dreams.

299 ★ Your friend's time is as valuable as your own and deserves as much respect.

300 ★ "A friend is, as it were, a second self."

—Cicero

301 ★ Friends discreetly let you know if your zipper is undone.

302 ★ Friends give back without asking.

303 ★ Friends won't make fun of you.

304 ★ Friendship can create a basis for world peace.

305 ★ Friends don't push each other to do things they don't want to do.

306 ★ Friends enhance, not control, our lives.

307 ★ A friend will always try to be kind to you.

308 ★ Share your toys.

309 ★ If you keep score, someone will end
up losing.

310 ★ Friends help us be better people.

311 ★ Don't help your friend hurt himself.

312 ★ "No person is useless while he or she has a friend."

—Robert Louis Stevenson

313 ★ A greater perspective of friendship is gained with age: disagreements are not as volatile; evenings are comfortably spent alone.

314 ★ But older people, like younger friends, must know they are loved.

315 ★ Send greeting cards or a gift at holidays to
all the friends you would like to receive one
from, and one to each relative who might
expect one from you.

316 ★ Cook your friend a special meal.

317 ★ Know when not to intrude.

318 ★ Be sympathetic.

319 ★ Build bridges instead of walls.

320 ★ Decide what is unforgivable.

321 ★ Share your grief.

322 ★ Friends make commitments to one another.
And make an extra effort to keep them.

323 ★ No-fault relationships are hollow.
Understand hurt and loss to feel love.

324 ★ Never ask a friend to compromise
her values.

325 ★ True friendship—like love—should be
unconditional.

326 ★ Celebrations are best when shared
with friends.

327 ★ A surprise party is worth the effort.

328 ★ "Doing nothing for others is the undoing
of ourselves."

—Horace Mann

329 ★ "True happiness consists not in the multitude of friends, but in their worth and choice."

—Ben Johnson

330 ★ Cultivate an optimistic outlook so you can bring joy to your friends, and vice versa.

331 ★ Take your friend on a nature walk to learn more about them.

332 ★ Plan a vacation around your friend's interests.

333 ★ When visiting a friend out of town, don't wear out your welcome.

334 ★ Friends shouldn't have to choose one over the other.

335 ★ No one is perfect.
Forgive each other's failings.

336 ★ "It is the peculiar quality of a fool to
perceive the faults of others and to forget
his own."   —Cicero

337 ★ "Friends are like fiddle strings, they must
not be screwed too tight."
                              —English proverb

338 ★ No one is always right.

339 ★ Friends let us act foolish, but don't tell us we are fools.

340 ★ True friends let you complain even when there's not a lot to complain about.

341 ★ But don't complain too often.

341 ★ Friends don't pry.

341 ★ "The nearer you come into a relation with
a person, the more necessary do tact and
courtesy become." —Holmes

344 ★ "A friend—one who knows all about you and loves you just the same."

—Elbert Hubbard

345 ★ It's okay if friends laugh when you sing.

346 ★ It's okay if a friend doesn't laugh at your corny jokes.

347 ★ What counts is what a friend does because she wants to, not what she has to.

348 ★ "It is sweet to be appreciated
by a great number and to be
understood by a few."

—Abel Binnard

349 ★ Friends can cry together.

350 ★ Friends uphold each other's pride, but keep each other's ego in check.

351 ★ Friends know when the other is full of it.

352 ★ Friends can offer constructive criticism.

353 ★ Friends don't stay mad for long. They admit their anger and work to dispel it.

354 ★ Some friendships need to ripen slowly.

355 ★ Old friends are like antiques—with care, they get better with age.

356 ★ Friends are not measured by the size
of their wallets.

357 ★ Friends are not measured by the
importance of their job titles.

358 ★ A good friend meter is the size of
their heart.

357 ★ Happiness is contagious.

360 ★ "A man, Sir, should keep his friendship in constant repair."

—Samuel Johnson

361 ★ Give your friend the benefit of the doubt.

362 ★ Pick today to contact an old friend and do
something special for them.

363 ★ Don't wait to lose a friend before you appreciate them.

364 ★ "Few people give themselves time to be friends."   —Robert Southery

365 ★ "Your friend is your needs
answered."

—Kahlil Gibran

<u>Favorites</u>

1.

2.

3.

Friends In Deed

4.

5.

6.